Table of Contents

Recipes to Make Thanksgiving More Amazing

Thanksgiving Hits Perfectly with the Best Thanksgiving Meals

BY: Ida Smith

License Notes

Introduction

Looking for the best delicacies to dazzle your friends, loved ones, and family members during Thanksgiving, you need not search further as this recipe book is here to present you with 30 amazing recipes and how to make them.

Turkey Gravy

Delicious and tasty!!

Preparation Time: 05 Minutes
Cooking Time: 10 Minutes
Yield: 6
List of Ingredients:

- – 2 cups turkey broth
- – 1 handful corn starch
- – 1 handful herbs (rosemary, sage, thyme, and parsley)
- – 4 tablespoons water
- – 1 tablespoon salt
- – 1 tablespoon pepper

Preparation:

1. Put the cornstarch in a bowl of water. Mix well and set aside.

2. Pour the turkey broth in a pot. Allowing boiling before you slowly add in the cornstarch mixture into the broth.

3. Add in the herbs, pepper, and salt. Serve and enjoy.

Heated Spiced Apple Cider Cocktail

Now, this is one cocktail recipe that you have never seen before.

Preparation Time: 03 Minutes

Cooking Times: 07 Minutes

Yield: 1

List of Ingredients:

- 1 cup red wine
- 6 tablespoons apple cider
- 4 tablespoons brandy
- 1 handful spices (cinnamon sticks and cardamom)
- 2 tablespoons honey
- 2 tablespoons orange juice

Preparation:

1. Add all the ingredients in a pot.
2. Cook for 5 minutes.
3. Allow cooling.
4. Serve.
5. Garnish with star anise and slices of orange.
6. Enjoy.

Glazed Carrots

It is high time you start seeing carrots more than that a bland vegetable you eat when you certainly want to get on a diet. With this recipe, you'd taste that carrots are so much more!

Preparation Time: 10 Minutes

Cooking Time: 10 Minutes

Yield: 2

List of Ingredients:

- 3 carrots (peeled, quartered, and halved)
- 1 tablespoon honey
- 4 tablespoons water
- 2 tablespoons oil
- 1 tablespoon pepper
- 1 tablespoon salt

Preparation:

1. Pour the oil in a pan.
2. Add in the carrots. Cook for 4 minutes.
3. Add in the pepper, salt, honey, and water.
4. Cook till the carrots begin to caramelize.
5. Serve. Garnish with the parsley

Cowboy Rice Salad

This rice salad is not only for cowboys; it's for the whole family!!

Preparation Time: 05 Minutes
Cooking Time: Nil
Yield: 4
List of Ingredients:

- 1 medium-sized red bell pepper (diced)
- 1 small-sized red onion (chopped)
- 1 green bell pepper (diced)
- 2 medium-sized tomatoes (diced)
- 7oz corn kernels (drained)
- 1 handful chopped cilantro
- 7oz black beans (rinsed and drained)

– 1 cup brown rice (cooked and drained)

Preparation:
1. Arrange all the ingredients in a bowl.
2. Mix well.
3. Serve.

Mac and Cheese

The Thanksgiving delicacy tastes better with this stovetop recipe.

Preparation Time: 05 Minutes

Cooking Time: 10 Minutes

Yield: 2

List of Ingredients:

- 2 tablespoons flour
- 1 cup water
- 2 tablespoons butter (unsalted)
- 1 cup milk
- 1 pinch salt
- 1 pinch black pepper
- 1 cup cheddar cheese (grated)
- 150g macaroni
- 40g mozzarella

Topping

- 1 pinch parsley
- 2 tablespoons grated cheese (Parmesan)
- 2 tablespoons breadcrumbs

Preparation:
1. Preheat the oven to 360 degrees F.
2. Put the butter in a frying pan.
3. Next, stir in the flour to form a thick paste.
4. Stir in the milk to dissolve the butter and flour.
5. Stir in the water, pepper, and salt. Add in the Mac.
6. Stir-cook the mixture for 1 minute.
7. Transfer the frying pan into the oven.
8. Bake till the Mac is cooked.
9. Next, after when you turn off the oven and turn on the broiler.
10. Add in the cheese.
11. Throw in a dash of parmesan cheese and panko.
12. Allow cooking for a few minutes.
13. Turn off the broiler. Allow cooling a bit before you serve.

Wild Rice Salad

Not only is this salad recipe delicious to taste, but it is also flavorful and colorful to crown your Thanksgiving table!

And to burst your bubbles, the ingredients to make this delicacy doesn't include the normal rice grain as the name suggests.

Shocked yet? Wait till you taste this delicious meal!

Preparation Time: 10 Minutes

Cooking Time: 15 Minutes

Yield: 2

List of Ingredients:

   – 1 handful pomegranate seeds
   – 75g wild rice (cooked al dente and drained)
   – 1 handful chopped baby rocket

- 1 handful chopped toasted pecans
- 1 handful green onions (sliced)
- 1 handful dried cranberries
- 50g Danish feta (crumbled and soft)

For the Dressing:

- 1 pinch black pepper
- 1 pinch salt
- 1 tablespoon wine vinegar (white)
- 1 pinch sugar
- 1 garlic clove (minced)
- 3 tablespoons olive oil

Preparation:
1. First, combine all the ingredients for your dressing in a bowl. Mix well.
2. Put the onions, wild rice, pomegranate, rocket, pecans, feta, and cranberries in a bowl.
3. Next, toss well.
4. Drizzle the dressing on it.
5. Mix well.
6. Serve and enjoy.

Pear cocktail

Your pears can feature in your Thanksgiving cocktail!

Preparation Time: 03 Minutes

Cooking Time: Nil

Yield: 1

List of Ingredients:

- 1 tablespoon St Germain
- 2 tablespoons champagne
- 1 tablespoon pear puree
- 1 tablespoon lemon juice
- 1 oz. dry gin

Preparation:

1. First, combine the entire ingredients in a cocktail shaker.
2. Shake vigorously.
3. Next, strain into your glass.
4. Top with pear slices.
5. Enjoy.

Roasted Butternut Squash Soup

This creamy comfort soup is healthy, delicious, and smooth!!!

Preparation Time: 10 Minutes

Cooking Time: 40 Minutes

Yield: 4

List of Ingredients:

- 1 small-sized butternut Squash (peeled, pitted, and chopped)
- 1 small-sized onion (Sliced)
- 1 medium-sized carrot (chopped)
- 2 stalks celery (chopped)
- 3 sprigs thyme (chopped)
- 3 sage leaves (chopped)
- 3 garlic cloves (minced)

– 1 handful chopped rosemary
– 2 cups vegetable stock
– 1 tablespoon olive oil
– 1 pinch cayenne red pepper (powder)
– 1 tablespoon pepper
– 1 tablespoon salt

Preparation:
1. Preheat the oven to 365 degrees F.
2. Put the chopped squash in a roasting pan.
3. Next, add the onions, garlic, celery, cloves, and carrots.
4. Add in the herbs, salt, pepper, red pepper, and olive oil.
5. Mix well.
6. Cook till all the vegetables are tender.
7. Next, put the cooked mixture in a food processor. Puree till the mixture is creamy and smooth.
8. Pour the mixture into a cooking pan. Add in the vegetable stock. Then, stir and allow to simmer for 5 minutes.
9. Serve.

Caramel Apple Mocktail

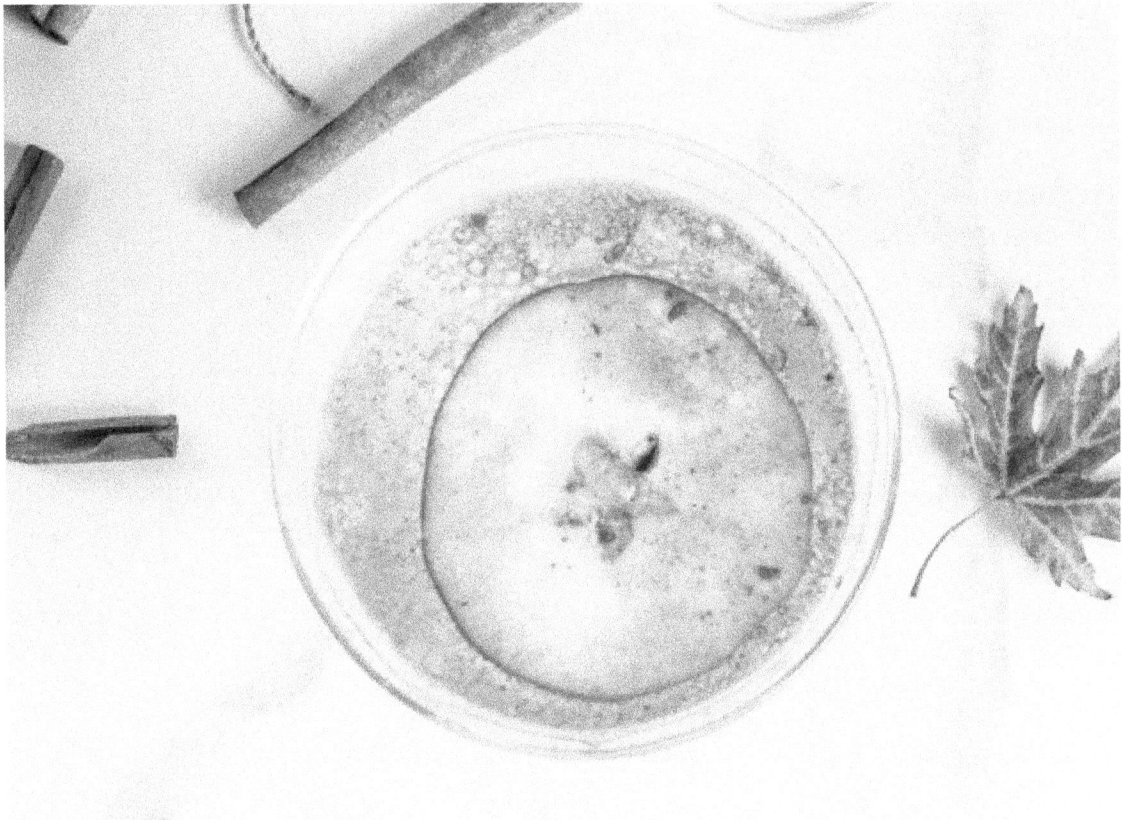

Something delicious and healthy for the kids this Thanksgiving!

Preparation Time: 02 Minutes

Cooking Time: Nil

Yield: 1

List of Ingredients:

- 1 handful ice cubes
- 1 oz. syrup (caramel)
- 1 handful sliced apples
- 2 oz. spiced apple cider
- 2 tablespoons caramel sauce

Preparation:

1. Coat your glass with a little of caramel sauce.

2. Add the rest of the ingredients asides the apple slices in a cocktail shaker. Shake well.
3. Serve into the prepared glass.
4. Top with more ice cubes and the apple slices.
5. Enjoy.

Cranberry Sauce

This delicious but not sugary sauce is the perfect pair for turkey.

Preparation Time: 05 Minutes

Cooking Time: 10 Minutes

Yield: 6

List of Ingredients:

- 250g fresh cranberries (divided)
- 4 tablespoons water
- 8 tablespoons sugar (white)
- 1 pinch salt
- 1 pinch lemon zest

Preparation:

1. Put the larger part of the cranberries in a pan of water. Add in the sugar, lemon, and salt. Cook till the berries have burst and the sugar has dissolved.

2. Add in the rest of the cranberries.

3. Cook for 3 more minutes. Serve.

Garlic Herb Roasted Carrots

You will actually never eat carrots the same way again!

Preparation Time: 05 Minutes
Cooking Time: 20 Minutes
Yield: 2
List of Ingredients:

- 1 tablespoon olive oil
- 1 pinch garlic powder
- 1 pinch thyme (dried)
- 5 medium-sized carrots (washed)
- 1 pinch pepper
- 1 pinch salt
- 1 pinch oregano (dried)
- 1 pinch parsley (dried)

– 1 pinch basil (dried)

Preparation:
1. Preheat your oven to 385 degrees F.
2. Grease a baking sheet with oil.
3. Combine the ingredients except for the carrots in a medium-sized mixing bowl.
4. Mix well.
5. Coat the carrots in the mixture.
6. Place the coated carrots on the baking sheet.
7. Bake till the carrots are tender.
8. Serve and enjoy.

Cranberry Walnut Apple Stuffing

Let's spice your stuffing up with some nut flavors, spices, and fruits!!!

Preparation Time: 10 Minutes

Cooking Time: 20 Minutes

Yield: 4

List of Ingredients:

- 1 handful diced apple
- 1 medium-sized onion (chopped)
- 1 tablespoon olive oil
- 1 loaf chopped bread (cranberry walnut)
- 1 tablespoon chopped rosemary
- 1 garlic clove (minced)
- 4 tablespoons heavy cream

- 1 medium-sized egg
- 4 tablespoons chicken stock
- 1 spray cooking spray
- 1 pinch black pepper (ground)
- 1 teaspoon salt

Preparation:
1. Preheat the oven to 385 degrees F.
2. Put the oil in a pan. Add in the onions, pepper, and salt.
3. Cook till the onions are sautéed.
4. Add in the apples. Cook till they are tender
5. Add in the rosemary and garlic.
6. Allow cooking for 2 minutes.
7. Turn down the heat.
8. Put the bread in a bowl. Add in the apple mixture.
9. Mix well. Put the chicken stock, cream, egg, pepper, and salt in a bowl. Mix well.
10. Transfer the mixture into the bread/apple mixture.
11. Pour the entire mixture in a coated baking pan. Bake for 20 minutes.
12. Serve.

Homemade Cream of Mushroom Soup

This mushroom soup is not earthy, but hearty and delicious!

Preparation Time: 05 Minutes

Cooking Time: 10 Minutes

Yield: 2

List of Ingredients:

- 1 teaspoon butter
- 4 tablespoons milk
- 4 tablespoons sliced mushrooms (white button)
- 1 tablespoon salt
- 1 tablespoon black pepper
- 4 tablespoons chicken broth
- 4 tablespoons flour

– 1 pinch garlic powder

– 1 pinch onion (powder)

Preparation:

1. Put the flour and milk in a bowl. Mix well.
2. Put the butter in a pot. Add in the mushrooms. Cook for 4 minutes.
3. Add in the onion, broth, and garlic.
4. Add in the flour and milk mixture.
5. Continue cooking until the mixture is thick.
6. Add in pepper and salt.
7. Serve.

Pumpkin Cake with Cream Cheese Frosting

Trust us; you don't actually want to miss this cake for your Thanksgiving dessert!

Preparation Time: 10 Minutes

Cooking Time: 20 Minutes

List of Ingredients:

- 2 medium-sized eggs
- 8 tablespoons canola oil
- 1 cup plain flour
- 10 tablespoons white sugar
- 220g pure pumpkin
- 1 teaspoon baking powder
- 1 tablespoon baking soda
- 1 tablespoon cinnamon powder

– 1 tablespoon salt

For the frosting

– 90g cream cheese
– 1 teaspoon vanilla extract
– 100g softened unsalted butter
– 2 cups icing sugar

Preparation:
1. Preheat your oven to 360 degrees F.
2. Next, line your baking pan with greased baking paper
3. Add in the sugar, eggs, pumpkin, and oil in a bowl.
4. Mix together.
5. Add in the rest of the ingredients. Mix thoroughly.
6. Next, pour and spread the mixture into the pan.
7. Bake for 20 minutes.
8. Transfer to a rack and allow cooling.
9. Add in the frosting ingredients in a bowl. Whisk well. Frost the cake with the frosting mixture.

Caramel Apple Martini

Martini tastes better with caramel and apple.

Preparation Time: 05 Minutes

Cooking Time: Nil

Yield: 1

List of Ingredients:

- 1 pinch salt
- 2 tablespoons caramel dessert topping
- 2 oz. apple cider
- 2 oz. vodka (caramel-infused)

Preparation:

1. First, coat the rim of your martini glass with caramel and salt.
2. Pour in the vodka and cider on a cocktail shaker.

3. Shake well.
4. Next, strain it into your prepared martini glass.
5. Top it with the dessert toppings.
6. Enjoy!

Lemon Potato Salad

We know a lot of you perceive potato salads to be boring, but we bet this healthy yet exciting recipe will change that notion for you!

Preparation Time: 10 Minutes
Cooking Time: Nil
Yield: 3
List of Ingredients:

- 1 pound baby potatoes (cooked, drained, and chit into sizes)
- 1 tablespoon fresh oregano (chopped)
- 1 tablespoon salt
- 1 tablespoon black pepper
- 4 scallions (Sliced)
- 1 tablespoon parsley (chopped)

– 1 cup salad dressing

Preparation:
1. Coat the potatoes in a bowl of dressing.
2. Place the coated potatoes in the fridge to chill.
3. Add in the rest of the ingredients.
4. Add in a little more dressing.
5. Serve.
6. Enjoy.

Cinnamon Maple Whiskey Sour

Whiskey lovers also have a cocktail recipe to celebrate Thanksgiving.

Preparation Time: 05 Minutes

Cooking Time: Nil

Yield: 1

List of Ingredients:

- 1 pinch cinnamon
- 1 tablespoon maple syrup
- 1 tablespoon lemon juice
- 2 tablespoons bourbon

Preparation:

1. Pour the ingredients in your shaker.
2. Next, shake well.

3. Then, strain the mixture into the glass of ice.
4. Enjoy.

Apple Salad with Cranberry and Candied Walnuts

Looking for the brightest, most flavored, tastiest, and most delicious salad recipe to showcase to your family, friends, and loved ones?

Actually, you can never go wrong with this recipe!!

Preparation Time: 10 Minutes

Cooking Time: 10 Minutes

Yield: 10

List of Ingredients:

- 2 red apples (deseeded, quartered, and sliced)
- 1 red onion (sliced)
- 1 lemon (juice)
- 8 handfuls chopped salad leaves (mixed)
- 1 tablespoon goat cheese (crumbled)

- 1 cup cranberries (boiled and drained)
- 1 cup salad dressing

For the candied nuts

- 1 cup walnuts
- 1 cup almond nuts
- 4 tablespoons sugar
- 2 tablespoons butter

Preparation:
1. Put the apple slices in a bowl. Add in a drizzle of lemon juice.
2. Put the butter in a pan. Add in the sugar.
3. Next, when it starts to bubble, add in the nuts.
4. Stir-fry till the nuts are toasted and candied. Transfer to a plate to cool off.
5. Add the salad leaves in a bowl.
6. Add in the rest of the ingredients.
7. Then, drizzle with the dressing.
8. Serve and enjoy!

Skinny Creamy Artichoke Soup

The perfect winter soup for your Thanksgiving celebration!

Preparation Time: 05 Minutes
Cooking Time: 25 Minutes
Yield: 2
List of Ingredients:

- 1 cup chicken stock
- 1 pinch salt
- 1 pinch black pepper
- 1 teaspoon olive oil
- 1 garlic clove (minced)
- 4 oz. artichoke hearts
- 1 teaspoon butter

- 2 small-sized potatoes (peeled and diced)
- 1 Leek (washed and Sliced)
- 1 handful chives
- 6 tablespoons heavy cream

Preparation:

1. Put the butter and oil in a pot. Add in the leeks. Cook and stir for 4 minutes. Add in the garlic. Cook for another 2 minutes.

2. Add in the potatoes. Cook for 4 minutes before you add in the artichoke.

3. Add in the salt, stock, and pepper. Cook for 15 minutes till the vegetables and potatoes are tender.

4. When the mixture is done. Allow it to cool.

5. Then you transfer it into a food processor.

6. Blend till smooth. Add in the cream. Mix well

7. Serve.

8. Garnish with chives.

9. Enjoy

Corn Salad and Avocado

The nutritional value asides, this corn salad recipe is so unusual but thrilling and delicious!!

Preparation Time: 10 Minutes

Cooking Time: 10 Minutes

Yield: 2

List of Ingredients:

- 200g cooked corn (drained)
- 1 tablespoon pepper
- 1 tablespoon salt
- 2 shallot (sliced)
- 1 avocado (pitted and halved)
- 100g cherry tomatoes (halved and diced)
- 1 lemon (juice)

- 1 handful chopped cilantro
- 2 tablespoons olive oil

Preparation:
1. Combine the entire ingredients in a large mixing bowl. Toss well.
2. Serve and enjoy.

Red Velvet Cake

Fluffy, soft, moist, and delicious!!!

Preparation Time: 15 Minutes
Cooking Time: 20 Minutes
Yield: 5
List of Ingredients:
Dry Ingredients:

- 1 pinch salt
- 1 pinch baking soda
- 1 tablespoon cocoa powder
- 200g plain flour

Wet Ingredients:

- 1 teaspoon vinegar (white)

- 150ml vegetable oil
- 50g soft butter (unsalted)
- 150g caster white sugar
- 1 egg
- 1 tablespoon food coloring (red)
- 1 tablespoon vanilla extract
- 150g buttermilk

Frosting

- 2 cups icing sugar (soft)
- 4 tablespoons soft butter (unsalted)
- 1 tablespoon vanilla extract
- 200g soft cream cheese

Preparation:
1. Preheat the oven to 365 degrees F.
2. Grease the cake pan with butter and cocoa powder.
3. Sieve the dry ingredients. Mix well.
4. Next, put sugar and butter in a bowl. Mix well.
5. Add in the eggs. Beat well till smooth.
6. Add in the oil, buttermilk, vanilla, food coloring, and vinegar in a bowl. Mix well till smooth.
7. Next, add in the dry ingredients into the bowl of wet ingredients.
8. Mix well. Pour the batter in a baking pan. Bake for 20 minutes. Set aside to cool.
9. Mix the frosting ingredients together. Frost the cake when it's cool. Serve and enjoy!

Crispy Smashed Potatoes

Crispy, fluffy, and delicious; all at once; so amazed balls!!

Preparation Time: 10 Minutes

Cooking Time: 30 Minutes

Yield: 6

List of Ingredients:

- 1 tablespoon pepper
- 1 tablespoon salt
- 350g potatoes (cooked and drained)
- 1 teaspoon olive oil
- 2 tablespoons butter (softened)

Preparation:

1. Preheat the oven to 355 degrees F.
2. Put the potatoes in a baking tray. Mash well. Set aside to dry a bit.
3. Add in a drizzle of butter.
4. Add in the olive oil
5. Followed by the pepper and salt.
6. Place the baking tray in the oven.
7. Bake till the mixture is golden crispy.
8. Serve immediately.

Apple Cider Mimosa

With just two ingredients, this mimosa has your Thanksgiving covered!

Preparation Time: 02 Minutes

Cooking Time: Nil

Yield: 1

List of Ingredients:

- 2 oz. champagne
- 2 small-sized apples (cider and slices)

Preparation:

1. Combine the ingredients in a glass.
2. Garnish with apple slices.

Creamy Cauliflower and Garlic Soup

Have you ever craved a soul that so tasty, delicious, and creamy for your Thanksgiving dinner? This recipe is literally the answer to your craving!!

Preparation Time: 10 Minutes

Cooking Time: 20 Minutes

Yield: 2

List of Ingredients:

- 2 tablespoons olive oil
- 1 small-sized onion (diced)
- 2 garlic cloves (peeled and minced)
- 1 medium-sized cauliflower head (cut)
- 1 cup chicken stock
- 1 handful Parmesan cheese (grated)

- 4 tablespoons half and half
- 1 tablespoon pepper
- 1 tablespoon salt

For toppings

- 1 handful Parmesan cheese
- 1 handful chopped thyme leaves

Preparation:

1. Pour the oil in a pot.
2. Add in the garlic, onion, and cauliflower. Cook for 10 minutes.
3. Add in the stock. Cook for another 5 minutes till the cauliflower is tender.
4. Pour the mixture in a blender till smooth.
5. Transfer the mixture back into the pot.
6. Add in the remaining part of the ingredients.
7. Serve.
8. Garnish with the toppings ingredient.
9. Enjoy.

Garlic Herb Butter Roast Turkey Breast

Another delicious way to treat your family and loved ones to an awesome serving of the legendary Thanksgiving turkey!!

Preparation Time: 10 Minutes

Cooking Time: 45 Minutes

Yield: 2

List of Ingredients:

- 3lb turkey breast
- 1 tablespoon salt
- 1 tablespoon black pepper
- 6 garlic cloves (smashed)
- 1 handful thyme, rosemary, and sage sprigs

For The Butter:

- 1 handful chopped parsley
- 1 handful chopped sage
- 1 handful chopped rosemary
- 1 handful chopped thyme leaves
- 2 garlic cloves (minced)
- 1 pinch black pepper
- 1 tablespoon salt
- 75g soft butter

Preparation:
1. Preheat the oven to 395 degrees F.
2. In your baking dish, add in the handful of herbs and the garlic.
3. To make your butter mixture. Combine the ingredients together and mix well.
4. Next, rub the butter mixture all over your turkey breast.
5. Put the turkey in the dish of herbs and garlic.
6. Set the turkey aside to marinate.
7. Season the breast with pepper and salt and place the baking dish inside the oven.
8. Then, bake the turkey till done.
9. Sieve out the herbs. Serve the turkey with the juices.

Corn Casserole

A Thanksgiving side dish that is utterly addictive and deliciously tasty!!

Preparation Time: 10 Minutes

Cooking Time: 30 Minutes

Yield: 5

List of Ingredients:

The dry Ingredients:

- 50g flour
- 1 pinch salt
- 20g sugar (white)
- 40g cornmeal (yellow)
- 1 pinch baking powder
- 1 pinch cayenne pepper

The wet Ingredients:

- 7 oz creamed corn
- 1 egg (beaten)
- 1 tablespoon canola oil
- 7 oz. can corn kernel
- 150g sour cream
- 70g melted butter (unsalted)

Preparation:
1. first, preheat your oven to 345 degrees F.
2. Second, put all the dry ingredients in a bowl. Mix well.
3. Do the same for the wet ingredients. Mix well.
4. Pour the dry ingredients mixture in the wet ingredients. Stir well.
5. Next, transfer the mixture into a casserole dish.
6. Bake till the top of the casserole is golden brown.
7. Serve immediately.

Mushroom Rice

Just for the love of mushrooms!!!

Preparation Time: 05 Minutes
Cooking Time: 10 Minutes
Yield: 4
List of Ingredients:

- 1 cup green onions (Sliced)
- 2 tablespoons canola oil (divided)
- 1 garlic clove (minced)
- 1 small-sized onion (diced)
- 1 tablespoon butter
- 400g mushrooms (Sliced)
- 1 cup uncooked rice (long grain)

– 2 cups chicken broth

Preparation:
1. Pour a half part of the oil in a pot. Add half part of the mushroom. Cook till golden.
2. Add in the pepper and salt. Cook for 2 minutes. Set aside.
3. Put another pot on the stove. Add in the butter and the oil. Add in the garlic and onions.
4. Next, add in the other half of the mushroom. Cook for 6 minutes.
5. Add in a dash of broth and the rice.
6. Then, mix well till the mixture is well combined.
7. Add in the remaining broth. Allow simmering and cook till the liquid dries up.
8. Add in the toasted mushroom and green onions.
9. Cover the pot and set aside for 8 minutes. Toss well. Serve and enjoy.

Rice Pilaf, Nuts, and Dried Fruits

A combination of rice, spices, fruits, and nuts makes the perfect Thanksgiving side meal.

Preparation Time: 05 Minutes

Cooking Time: 15 Minutes

Yield: 2

List of Ingredients:

- 1 tablespoon olive oil
- 2 handfuls shelled pistachios (toasted)
- 1 garlic clove (minced)
- 1 handful almonds (silvered and toasted)
- 1 small-sized onion (chopped)
- 60g basmati rice (uncooked)
- 200ml chicken broth
- 2 handfuls dried apricots
- 2 handfuls raisins

– 1 handful chopped parsley

Spices:

– 1 pinch black pepper
– 1 pinch cumin (ground)
– 1 pinch cardamom
– 1 pinch ground cinnamon

Preparation:
1. Put the oil in a pan. Add in the onion and garlic.
2. Allow sautéing for 2 minutes.
3. Next, add in the rice and stir for 1 minute.
4. Add in the spices, raisins, broth, and apricots. Stir well. Cook for 20 minutes.
5. When it's done and liquid-free, fluff rice with a fork.
6. Then, stir in the toasted nuts.
7. Serve.
8. Garnish with parsley.

Cranberry Margarita

When you think a sauce is all you can make with your cranberries and BOOM! This recipe says no!!

Preparation Time: 05 Minutes

Cooking Time: Nil

Yield: 5

List of Ingredients:

- 1 squeeze of lemon juice
- 1 cup liqueur (orange-flavored)
- 2 cups cranberry juice
- 6 tablespoons tequila

Preparation:

1. Add in all your ingredients in a glass.
2. Mix well and serve.

3. Top with a handful of fresh cranberries and ice cubes.
4. Enjoy.

Arugula Salad with Pecan and Apple

A salad that would make your Thanksgiving table look so delicious!

Preparation Time: 05 Minutes

Cooking Time: Nil

Yield: 2

List of Ingredients:

- 2 handfuls feta cheese (crumbled)
- 2 oz. baby arugula
- 2 handfuls pecans (candied)
- 1 medium-sized apple (Sliced)
- 4 tablespoons vinaigrette dressing

Preparation:

1. Add in the first 4 ingredients in a bowl.
2. Drizzle in the dressing.
3. Serve and enjoy.

Conclusion

Thanksgiving is here. This is the best time to show your loved one some special culinary skills, and you have this Cookbook to help you achieve them without worries and stress.

Have a beautiful and wonderful Thanksgiving!

Don't miss out!

Visit the website below and you can sign up to receive emails whenever Ida Smith publishes a new book. There's no charge and no obligation.

https://books2read.com/r/B-A-LRXL-WMOIB

BOOKS 2 READ

Connecting independent readers to independent writers.

Also by Ida Smith

Soothing Vietnamese Dishes You Can Enjoy with Friends: Hanoi Inspired Recipes for Your Special Friendly Hangouts

Easy Recipes for NBA Lovers: Make Your Kitchen Come Alive with These NBA Meals

Easy Salad and Dinner Recipes You Can Make Anytime: Salad and Dinner Recipes That Go Together

Meat and Pasta Recipes You Should Try: Spice Up Your Taste Bud with This Amazing Combination of Meat and Pasta

The Perfect Green Pesto to Jazz Up Any Dish: Cooking with Pesto – 30 Ways to Get It Right

Tiktok Dishes That Can Be Made In 30 Minutes: Viral Recipes to Include in Your Tiktok Videos

Delicious Recipes to Cook with Kids: Make Your Kids Smile with These Meals

Quick and Easy Breakfast for Dinner Recipes: Easy Breakfast Meals That Will Sub Perfectly for Dinner

Recipes to Make Thanksgiving More Amazing: Thanksgiving Hits Perfectly with the Best Thanksgiving Meals

The Perfect Recipes to Get Your Party Started: Get Your Party Started with These Amazing Recipes

The Recipe Book for Game Time Meals: Get the Family & Friends Ready for some Pretty Game Meals

Tex-Mex Recipes That You Can't Do Without: Half Mexican, Half Texas: Pure Delight!

Unique Ice Cream Recipes to Try at Home: 30 Around the World Ice Cream Recipes to Try Now

Best and Most Tasty African and American Recipe Combos: Flavoursome African and American recipe Combos That Will Set Your Taste Buds on Fire

Dessert Recipes that You Can Bank on: The Best Meals to Wrap up Your Menus!

Easy Stockpot Recipes for The Family: Easy Recipes for Your Kitchen

Get Your Salsa Groove on with These Recipes: Dance and Dine with The Best Mexican Recipes

Wonderful Pies Recipe for Thanksgiving Table: Kick-Start your Thanksgiving Table With these Delicious Recipes

Kid-Friendly Veggie Recipes for Healthy Kids: Recipes That Will Keep Your Kids Healthy

Super Italian Recipes Is Coming to Your Kitchen: If You Are in Doubt, Go Italian!

The World of Cooking Recipes: Recipes That Will Make You Travel Around

Easy Lemon Recipes for All Season: Lemon-Inspired Recipes for Your Family

Sauce Recipes to Spice Up Your Food!: Sauces Make the World Go Rounder Than Round!

Sweet Corn Recipes You Can Enjoy in Your Backyard: The Corn Recipes for The Corn Lovers Out There!

Easy Chinese Dumpling Recipes: Dumpling Recipe for everyone

Foil Meal for Winter Days: Cooking with Foil – Your Way to Less Cleaning

Paella and Side Dishes That Go Well with Paella: The Best Paella Recipes for You and Your Family!

Amazing Brunch Recipes You Can't Resist: Brunch Recipes for A Lazy Day

Asian and Caribbean Recipes to Explore: It Gets Better in Doubles!

Best Brunch In LA: LA Brunch – The Best Way to Enjoy the City of Angels

Best Recipes for Pool Parties: Tasty Recipes for Your Wonderful Pool Party

Chicken Recipes That Make You Feel Like A Pro Chef: Chicken Recipes You Must Try Today

Instant Recipes in a Jar for Your Trips and Picnics: Recipes just Got Better with a Jar!

Irresistible Barbeque Recipes: Easy to Prepare Smoker Recipes that You can't Resist

Main and Side Cheese Recipes to Crave: Don't Crave It till You Cheese It!

Pastries for The Pastries Loving You: Classic Pastries That Take You to The English And French Countrysides

Unusual Weight Loss Recipes that You Don't Know About: Your Weight Loss Plan can be Exciting and Delicious, You Know Right?

Winter Soup Recipes You Would Always Love: Great Soups Recipes to Try out in the Cold Days

Crowd-Pleaser Appetizers and Cocktails to Die For: Best Recipes ever of Appetizers and Cocktails

Vegan Dishes for Meat Lovers: Tasty Vegan Recipes for Meat Lovers

DIY Skin Butter to Moisturize Dry and Itchy Skin: Restore and Revive Dry &Itchy Skin with Homemade Body Butter

Recipes That Enhance Your Cravings for More: These Recipes Will Get You Addicted to Them!

DIY Facial Scrubs for Clear and Glowing Skin: Simple and Organic DIY Face Scrub

Unique Greece Island Recipes You Must Try: From the Island to the Table - Recipes for every Family

Classic Indian Recipes for You and Your Special One: Perfect Recipes for You and Your Special One!

Easy Homemade Soaps That Save You the Dollars: Personalize Your Character in a Handmade Soap

Instant Homemade Shampoos That Work for Natural Hair: Simple Homemade Shampoo Recipes for Your Natural Hair

Keep Your Family Closer with Traditional Amish Recipes: Home Is Where Good Food Is

Asian Takeout You can Make at Home: Asian Takeout Meals that Are Not Take-Outs!

Easy Organic Recipes for a Glowing Skin; DIY Skin Solutions: DIY Skin Glow Recipes

Homemade Hair Conditioners from your Surrounding: Treat your Hair like your Food – Simple Conditioners You Can Make at Home

Recipes That Won't Make You Miss Excess Sugar: Healthy Meals Send the Doctor Away!

Simple and Delicious Meals That Will Create a Japanese Kitchen in Your House: Japanese Recipes That Everyone Will Love

Easily Found Natural Ingredients to Get Rid of Fine Lines: Recipes Made with Ingredients from your Pantry for Flawless Skin

Slower Cooker - Wholesome Recipes for the Family: Slow Cooker Recipes the Family Will Enjoy

Wok Recipes to Keep You Warm: Wok Dishes - Bringing Flavors to Every Meal

www.ingramcontent.com/pod-product-compliance
Lightning Source LLC
Chambersburg PA
CBHW081300040426
42452CB00014B/2582